WRITIN

BY
ROBERT KERR and EDWARD PRESTON

ILLUSTRATED BY
STEVEN VARBLE

COPYRIGHT © 1993 Mark Twain Media, Inc.

Printing No. CD-1851

Mark Twain Media Inc., Publishers
Distributed by Carson-Dellosa Publishing Company, Inc.

The

Writing

Organization

Research

Doing it all

Is . . .

fully reproducible lessons, activities, and projects designed to guide students through the writing process, develop critical thinking skills, improve decision-making abilities, and increase enjoyment of language through different kinds of media.

Contents

The Word is...Research:

The Word is...Doing It All: by amplifying skills and knowledge

The

Writing

O

R

D

Is . . .

Part I

The Word Is...Writing

The word is WRITING. In other words, communication. Sharing facts and feelings is the very purpose of writing. This section of the workbook is devoted to four types of written communication: descriptive, process, narrative, and creative, and it also includes a section on sentence and paragraph development. Each form will include exercises for students of varying skill levels.

Descriptive writing should be concrete, using exact details that create the desired image. Students should learn the value of lively verbs, appropriate nouns, and vivid adjectives. Descriptive writing is, in fact, fundamental to narrative and creative.

Another important fundamental aspect of narrative and creative writing is process writing, an extremely disciplined form. In process writing, the student must move from one point to another using some type of logical order. Again, vigorous verbs and solid nouns will help to keep the product lively.

Narrative writing, one of the oldest forms of communication, gives an account or tells a story. It is close to the sequential point-by-point approach found in process writing. The difference is that the writer has more freedom in the narrative, yet preciseness and clarity must be maintained.

The element of freedom is even more prevalent in creative writing. Essentially imaginative, creative writing is difficult to "teach." Instead, the teacher can concentrate on inspiration, guidance, and encouragement. Young writers need to be praised for their successes and encouraged to put dreams and visions into words.

2

Show, Not Tell

The word is <u>show,</u> not <u>tell</u>. This section of the book is devoted to the development of sentences and paragraphs which express feelings and appeal to the senses rather than merely tell something.

The first exercise invites students to expand the subject of a very basic sentence by adding vivid adjectives, appropriate prepositional phrases, and for more advanced writers, verb forms and appositives. Students will also have the opportunity to combine any of those elements. Here is an example:

BASIC: The dog ran.
                The shaggy, mangy dog ran. (adjectives)
                The dog, frightened by the truck, ran. (verb form)
                The dog with the white tail ran. (preposition)
                The shaggy, mangy dog, frightened by the truck, ran. (combination)

The next exercise asks students to expand the verb in the sentence, using lively adverbs and prepositional phrases. Remember to remind students that adverbs and adverb phrases tell <u>when, where,</u> and <u>how</u>.

BASIC: The dog ran.
                The dog ran wildly. (adverb)
                The dog ran down the street. (preposition)
                The dog ran wildly down the street. (combination)

The final exercise deals with expanding the rest of the sentence, especially objects, by once again using adjectives, prepositions, and verb forms.

BASIC: The dog chased the cat.
                The dog chased the neighbor's yellow cat. (adjectives)
                The dog chased the cat up the tree. (preposition)
                The dog chased the neighbor's yellow cat up the tree. (combination)

Name _____

SHOW, NOT TELL

EXPAND THE **SUBJECT**

DIRECTIONS: For each of the basic sentences in this exercise, expand the subject by using adjectives, prepositional phrases, and verb forms. The first one is done for you.

1. BASIC: The phone rang.

   (adjectives)   The white cordless phone rang.

   (preposition)   The phone in the kitchen rang.

   (verb form)   The phone lying on the table rang.

   (combine)   The white cordless phone lying on the table in the kitchen rang.

2. BASIC: The horses grazed.

   (adjectives)   _____

   (preposition)   _____

   (verb form)   _____

   (combine)   _____

3. BASIC: The children swam.

   (adjectives)   _____

   (preposition)   _____

   (verb form)   _____

   (combine)   _____

Name _____

EXPAND THE SUBJECT (CONTINUED)

4. BASIC: The team played. _____

    (adjectives)   _____

    (preposition)   _____

    (verb form)   _____

    (combine)   _____

5. BASIC: The wind blew. _____

    (adjectives)   _____

    (preposition)   _____

    (verb form)   _____

    (combine)   _____

6. BASIC: The flames rose. _____

    (adjectives)   _____

    (preposition)   _____

    (verb form)   _____

    (combine)   _____

7. BASIC: The plane landed. _____

    (adjectives)   _____

    (preposition)   _____

    (verb form)   _____

    (combine)   _____

Name _____

SHOW, NOT TELL

EXPAND THE **VERB**

DIRECTIONS:

For each of the basic sentences below, expand the verb by using adverbs and prepositions. The first one is done for you.

1. BASIC: The phone rang.

    (adverbs)   The phone rang constantly.

    (prepositions)   The phone rang throughout the night.

    (combine)   The phone rang constantly throughout the night.

2. BASIC: The horses grazed.

    (adverbs)   _____

    (prepositions)   _____

    (combine)   _____

                      _____

3. BASIC: The children swam.

    (adverbs)   _____

    (prepositions)   _____

    (combine)   _____

                      _____

6

Name _____

EXPAND THE VERB (continued)

4. BASIC: The team played.

   (adverbs) _____

   (prepositions) _____

   (combine) _____

   _____

   _____

5. BASIC: The wind blew.

   (adverbs) _____

   (prepositions) _____

   (combine) _____

   _____

   _____

6. BASIC: The flames rose.

   (adverbs) _____

   (prepositions) _____

   (combine) _____

   _____

   _____

7. BASIC: The plane landed.

   (adverbs) _____

   (prepositions) _____

   (combine) _____

   _____

   _____

Name _____

EXPAND AND COMBINE

DIRECTIONS: Using the same basic sentences as in the first two exercises, combine your expanded subjects and verbs. If you used several adjectives, adverbs, or phrases, you may want to omit or move one of them in order to maintain a smooth sentence.

   HELPFUL NOTE: Keep words and phrases that were used to expand the subject as close to the subject as possible. On the other hand, adverbs and phrases used to expand the verb can be moved to other places in the sentence. The first example from the previous exercises is expanded for you. Note the movement of the phrase used to expand the verb.

1. BASIC: The phone rang.
            Throughout the night, the white cordless phone lying on the table rang. _____

2. BASIC: The horses grazed.
            _____

            _____

3. BASIC: The children swam.
            _____

            _____

4. BASIC: The team played.
            _____

            _____

5. BASIC: The wind blew.
            _____

            _____

6. BASIC: The flames rose.
            _____

            _____

7. BASIC: The plane landed.
            _____

            _____

Name _____

EXPANDING A SENTENCE WITH AN OBJECT

If you had no trouble expanding the subjects and verbs in the first three exercises, try expanding the object in a sentence. Remember that the object follows an action verb and answers **WHAT** to the verb.

EXAMPLE: The dog ate the bone. (bone is the object; it tells what the dog ate)

DIRECTIONS: For each of the following sentences, expand the subject, verb, and object by using at least one adjective, adverb, or phrase. The first one is done for you.

1. BASIC: The carpenter dropped a hammer.
    The elderly carpenter accidentally dropped a new hammer from the roof.

2. BASIC: The class will write reports.

    _____

    _____

    _____

3. BASIC: Workers built shelters.

    _____

    _____

    _____

4. BASIC: The teacher placed the book.

    _____

    _____

    _____

5. BASIC: The policeman directed the traffic.

    _____

    _____

    _____

Name _____

EXPANDING THE OBJECT (continued)

5. BASIC: The thief stole jewels.

_____

_____

_____

6. BASIC: The maid placed the vase.

_____

_____

_____

7. BASIC: Kids ate food.

_____

_____

_____

8. BASIC: The custodian swept the floor.

_____

_____

_____

9. BASIC: A mechanic repaired the engine.

_____

_____

_____

Name _____

EXPANDING THE OBJECT (continued)

10. BASIC: The artist painted the portrait.

_____

_____

_____

11. BASIC: The coach gave instructions.

_____

_____

_____

12. BASIC: The boy found a wallet.

_____

_____

_____

13. BASIC: Cooks prepared a meal.

_____

_____

_____

14. BASIC: A soldier saved lives.

_____

_____

_____

Name _____

SHOW, NOT TELL

THE PARAGRAPH

DIRECTIONS: Expand the basic sentences into a paragraph that creates a picture by appealing to the senses. Read the example carefully. Does the paragraph affect touch, hearing, sight, smell, or taste?

1.　The dinner was enjoyable.

　　Laughter and the smell of turkey and dressing filled the air as twenty members of my family ate Thanksgiving dinner together. Stories of past holidays and other memories were shared from table to table. At the same time, mouth-watering salads, creamy-smooth mashed potatoes and hot gravy, and moist slices of delicious turkey were passed from plate to plate.

2.　The best player was nervous.

_____

_____

_____

_____

_____

_____

_____

_____

_____

_____

_____

_____

_____

Name _____

EXPANDING THE PARAGRAPH (continued)

3.   The girl was excited.

_____

_____

_____

_____

_____

_____

_____

_____

4.   They were good dancers.

_____

_____

_____

_____

_____

_____

_____

_____

EXPANDING THE PARAGRAPH (continued)

5.   The party was terrific.

_____

_____

_____

_____

_____

_____

_____

_____

6.   The sunset was beautiful.

_____

_____

_____

_____

_____

_____

_____

_____

Name _____

EXPANDING THE PARAGRAPH (continued)

7.   The present was a surprise.

_____

_____

_____

_____

_____

_____

_____

_____

8.   A mother was worried.

_____

_____

_____

_____

_____

_____

_____

_____

Descriptive Writing

INTRODUCTION:

Descriptive writing involves the senses. By choosing the best verbs, adjectives, nouns, and adverbs, the writer creates an image that the reader can actually see, feel, hear, taste, or smell.

More advanced writers should be encouraged to create mood through the use of colorful adjectives. Also, students can accent spatial order–that is, describing from one point to another by clearly explaining the relation of position.

Finally, encourage the use of transitional words and phrases in writing descriptively. Here are some possible choices:

Transitional Words and Phrases			
in	over	beneath	around
on	below	beside	against
above	onto	down	side by side
under	inside	by	in back of
behind	ahead of	toward	
near	between	among	

INSTRUCTIONS:

The story starters found on the following pages can be duplicated, laminated, and separated for classroom use. You can assign topics or allow students either to draw randomly or to select their own. A blank page has also been included for your own topics. Another Descriptive Writing project follows the story starter pages.

AN APPROACHING STORM

What do you see?

What do you hear?

What might you smell?

THE EMPTY FARM HOUSE

What is outside?

What is inside?

What do you hear?

AUTOGRAPH HUNTERS

How many are there?

Where are they?

How do they act?

AN OIL SPILL

Where is it?

How big is it?

What damage has it done?

A HOUSE THAT
SANTA WON'T ENTER

Where is it?

Who lives there?

Why won't Santa enter?

MY BEST FRIEND

What good qualities?

What special interests?

What do you have in common?

MY CLASSROOM

What does it look like?

What sounds would be heard?

How are the seats arranged?

OVERNIGHT CAMPOUT

What do you see?

What do you hear?

What might you smell?

A FAMILY TRADITION

When is it done?

Who is involved?

What happens?

A BROTHER/SISTER

How old?

Good qualities?

Bad qualities?

A FAMOUS RELATIVE

Who is this person?

What has made this person famous?

How do you feel around this person?

MY HERO

Who is it?

Why do you look up to this person?

What has this person done?

A SUMMER CARNIVAL

What do you see?

What do you hear?

What do you smell?

What do you feel?

A VACATION SPOT

Where is it?

What does it look like?

What do you do there?

YOUR ROOM

What is in it?

What sounds might exist?

How do you feel in it?

What makes it YOU?

FAVORITE HOLIDAY

What is it?

Why do you like it?

How does it make you feel?

Very Important People

How would you describe your parents, grandparents, best friend? There are probably many things that you could say about these people and why they are important to your life. Here's your chance to do so.

Imagine that either your mom, dad, grandmother, grandfather, or best friend has been nominated for a Nobel Prize. This is an award recognized throughout the whole world. You have the job of describing why this person should win this award. Your description should tell the things about this person that make her or him so special that he or she deserves the Nobel Prize.

The form below has been sent to you from Stockholm, Sweden, where the committee will meet to choose the Nobel Prize. Fill it out to help them decide on a winner. You can choose which person to describe: mom, dad, grandparent, best friend.

Nobel Prize Nomination for _____
                                             (WRITE IN CATEGORY)

Person nominated : _____

Why this person should win the Nobel prize:

Nominator's Name _____

Process Writing

INTRODUCTION:

The "how to" process should be clear and accurate. Process writing is a step-by-step approach that is simple yet specific. More advanced writers can experiment with the concept of relationship. That means that if one step affects another, that relationship must be explained.

Transitions and phrases can be used effectively in this process. Possible examples are:

Transitional Words and Phrases		
first	next	when
second	last	until
third	then	finally
fourth	now	to start with
at first	at last	

A basic pattern to organize the process paper could be:

1. Select the topic
2. Brainstorm related steps
3. Put steps in a logical order
4. Convert steps into sentences
5. Add transitions and a good opening sentence

INSTRUCTIONS:

Duplicate the example page for a process paper. An opening sentence and transitions are provided. Students can add the details. The following pages contain several topics for use in a process assignment. Duplicate, laminate, and separate the topics for classroom use. Assign topics or allow students to draw or choose their own. A blank page has been added at the end of the activity for your own topics.

FOLLOW-UP:

The process paper is an excellent lead-in to "how to" speeches.

21

HOW I PREPARE FOR SCHOOL
For me, getting ready for school is no easy

task. First _____

_____

_____. Next _____

_____

_____

_____. Then _____

_____

_____. Later _____

_____

_____. Finally _____

_____ .

PROCESS PAPER TOPICS

HOW TO STOP THE HICCUPS	HOW TO OPERATE A FAVORITE COMPUTER GAME
HOW TO PUT ON A BICYCLE CHAIN	HOW TO MAKE A MONSTER SANDWICH
HOW TO BUILD A BIRDHOUSE	HOW TO START A CAMP FIRE
HOW TO TREAT A BURN OR BITE	HOW TO PREPARE A FAVORITE RECIPE

PROCESS PAPER TOPICS

HOW TO LOCATE A CITY ON A MAP	HOW TO OPERATE A VIDEO CAMERA
HOW TO SOLVE A PUZZLE OR CRYPTOGRAM	HOW TO SET A DINNER TABLE
HOW HONEY IS MADE	HOW TO BAKE A CAKE
HOW TO FISH FOR BASS / CATFISH / SUNFISH	HOW TO PITCH A TENT

PROCESS PAPER TOPICS

HOW SLEET IS FORMED	HOW TO PREPARE AND FLY A KITE
HOW TO WATER SKI	HOW TO SWIM A CERTAIN STROKE
HOW TO COLLECT SPORTSCARDS	HOW TO PLAY AN OUTSIDE TEAM SPORT
HOW TO PLAY A BOARD GAME	HOW TO PLAY AN INSIDE TEAM SPORT

PROCESS PAPER TOPICS

HOW TO PUT TOGETHER A MODEL	HOW TO TAKE BLOOD PRESSURE
HOW TO CARE FOR A HOUSE PET	HOW TO USE LIFE-SAVING SKILLS
HOW TO PACK A SUITCASE	HOW TO PUT OUT A FIRE PROPERLY
HOW TO BRUSH YOUR TEETH PROPERLY	HOW TO PLAN A PARTY

PROCESS PAPER TOPICS

HOW PYRAMIDS WERE BUILT	HOW TO PLANT FLOWERS
HOW TO USE A WOODBURNING TOOL	HOW TO TAKE CARE OF A LAWN MOWER
HOW TO SEW WITH A PATTERN	HOW TO RUN A LEMONADE STAND
HOW TO PAINT A ROOM	HOW TO SHOP FOR BARGAINS

TEACHER TOPICS

Narrative Writing

INTRODUCTION:

The narrative is, in effect, a natural way of writing. The accent should be on the order of events. Young writers can easily use a natural time sequence, especially writing from personal experience. Students should be encouraged to use a strong, lively opening sentence. By asking questions like Why? Where? When? How? and Who? the writer can develop the necessary details to produce a quality paper. Finally, encourage the use of transitional words such as the following:

Transitional Words and Phrases			
first	now	when	by the time
then	soon	before	next
later	after		

INSTRUCTIONS:

Duplicate, laminate, and separate the story helps on the following pages. Assign topics or allow students to select or draw their own. A blank page has been included for your own topics.

Following the story starters are worksheets with which students may develop narrative writing skills as they examine their experiences with emotions.

29

Things were fine until I realized I had the wrong...

(Complete the sentence and finish the story on your own paper.)

It wasn't really my fault, but...

(Complete the sentence and finish the story on your own paper.)

The day I became a hero happened when...

(Complete the sentence and finish the story on your own paper.)

I realized that being the oldest/ youngest child had its disadvantages when...

(Complete the sentence and finish the story on your own paper.)

There was no doubt that I had a close call after...

(Complete the sentence and finish the story on your own paper.)

The most important decision I ever made in my life was when...

(Complete the sentence and finish the story on your own paper.)

I can truly say that being sick can really be fun because...

(Complete the sentence and finish the story on your own paper.)

I proved to my friends that I was quick on my feet when...

(Complete the sentence and finish the story on your own paper.)

STORY STARTERS – Narrative Writing

I was in a real big hurry, and suddenly...

(Complete the sentence and finish the story on your own paper.)

I never thought I would get the last laugh until...

(Complete the sentence and finish the story on your own paper.)

My conscience was my guide the day that...

(Complete the sentence and finish the story on your own paper.)

If I could have had only five more minutes then...

(Complete the sentence and finish the story on your own paper.)

The day I would most like to forget was when...

(Complete the sentence and finish the story on your own paper.)

I found out that words can indeed be cheap when...

(Complete the sentence and finish the story on your own paper.)

I did not realize that what I was about to do would set an example for others.

(Finish the story on your own paper.)

I found out that I have a real nose for news after...

(Complete the sentence and finish the story on your own paper.)

TEACHER TOPICS

32

Name _____

FEAR

Share about a time when you really felt afraid. Where were you? What was happening? How did you handle your fear? What was the result of your dealing with it? What did you learn from it?

_____

_____

_____

_____

_____

_____

_____

_____

_____

_____

_____

_____

_____

_____

_____

_____

_____

_____

Name _____

ANGER

Tell about a time when you felt angry. What had happened? Did you feel at the time that you had the right to be angry? Do you feel the same way today? Why or why not? Could the problem have been handled differently? If so, what would you have done?

_____

_____

_____

_____

_____

_____

_____

_____

_____

_____

_____

_____

_____

_____

_____

_____

_____

_____

_____

Name _____

LONELINESS

Describe a time in your life when you felt alone. Where were you at the time? Did you have any other feelings other than loneliness? What caused you to feel separated and by yourself? What did you learn from this experience? What took away the lonely feeling?

_____

_____

_____

_____

_____

_____

_____

_____

_____

_____

_____

_____

_____

_____

_____

_____

_____

_____

_____

_____

Name _____

EXCITEMENT

Relate a moment in your life when you felt the greatest excitement. What had happened? Who else was involved? Did others feel the same excitement? Have you felt that way since that time? If so, when and where?

_____

_____

_____

_____

_____

_____

_____

_____

_____

_____

_____

_____

_____

_____

_____

_____

_____

_____

_____

Name _____

EMBARRASSMENT

Tell about a time when you were completely embarrassed. What had taken place that made you feel this way? What did you do to deal with the situation? Do you think that you handled it the best way? Why or Why not?

_____

_____

_____

_____

_____

_____

_____

_____

_____

_____

_____

_____

_____

_____

_____

_____

_____

_____

_____

Creative Writing

INTRODUCTION:

Creative writing contains elements of the narrative and descriptive styles. It offers the writer a freedom in which to operate and a fresh environment in which to formulate thoughts and ideas. Use your own judgment as to evaluating mechanics. It should be noted, however, that too much emphasis on mechanics can hinder the creative process in the younger writer.

Older or more advanced writers would benefit from experimenting with metaphor, personification, and other literary devices. Anything goes in creative writing!

INSTRUCTIONS:

The following six pages are single-page story topics with prompts. These are particularly appropriate for use with younger students. Following these pages are the story starter pages. Duplicate, laminate, and separate the creative writing topics on these pages. Assign the topics or allow students to select or randomly draw their own. A blank page has been included for your own topics.

This section ends with "What If's" activities. These are explained more fully on page 48.

IF I COULD BE AN ANIMAL FOR ONE DAY

People say that animals have easy lives. I would like to try living like an animal just for one day.

If I had the chance I would be a _____ .

(finish the sentence and tell what your day would be like)

_____

_____

_____

_____

_____

_____

_____

_____

_____

_____

_____

_____

_____

_____

_____

_____

_____

_____

(use your own paper if you need to)

MY GREAT INVENTION

Inventions are created when people have a need for something. I know exactly what our (house, school, country) needs.

_____

_____

_____

_____

_____

_____

_____

_____

_____

_____

_____

_____

_____

_____

_____

_____

_____

(use your own paper if you need to)

PRINCIPAL FOR A DAY

If I had the chance to run my school for one day, I know I would make a few changes. It would be fun to be principal of my school for a day.

_____

_____

_____

_____

_____

_____

_____

_____

_____

_____

_____

_____

_____

_____

_____

_____

_____

_____

(use your own paper if you need to)

Creative Writing

Name _____

THE TIME CAPSULE

As I crawled under my front porch after my baseball, I noticed a loose brick in the foundation of the house. When I tried to shove the brick back in, two more bricks fell out, revealing a large tin can sealed at the top. I brought it out in the light, opened the top, and found some of the weirdest things I had ever seen.

_____

_____

_____

_____

_____

_____

_____

_____

_____

_____

_____

_____

_____

_____

_____

_____

_____

_____

(use your own paper if you need to)

SURPRISE AT THE DOOR

The doorbell rang and I ran to see who was there. I opened the door, but I couldn't see anyone. Suddenly I looked down at the porch step and saw a box. I removed the top and to my surprise saw

_____.

(finish the line and explain what happened)

_____

_____

_____

_____

_____

_____

_____

_____

_____

_____

_____

_____

_____

_____

_____

_____

(use your own paper if you need to)

THE FORGOTTEN HOUR

My mother had told me to be home at five o'clock. I left my friend's house down the street in plenty of time. However, when I entered my house the clock said six o'clock, and no one was home.

_____

_____

_____

_____

_____

_____

_____

_____

_____

_____

_____

_____

_____

_____

_____

_____

_____

(use your own paper if you need to)

WHY I WOULD LIKE TO BE A _____ (object / animal)	IF I WON A $1000 SHOPPING SPREE
MAN'S GREATEST INVENTION	MORE THAN JUST A YARD SALE
A SECOND CHANCE	WAKING UP SOMEWHERE ELSE
ONE MORE WAS TOO MANY	PLACE A NURSERY RHYME CHARACTER IN A MODERN SETTING

HISTORY REPEATS ITSELF ONCE AGAIN	A ROCK SPEAKS OF ITS HISTORY (or change "rock" to another word))
AN OLD MYSTERY NOW SOLVED	THE INNOCENT BYSTANDER
THE VOICE STILL HEARD	HOW _____ WAS DISCOVERED
BEST FRIEND, BIGGEST RIVAL	THE UNKEPT SECRET

WRITING ABOUT WHAT-IF'S

INTRODUCTION:

Students often do their best creative writing when they are presented with a question that is challenging. One of the most challenging of questions is the "What if.." variety. On the following pages are several questions which could have both a positive view and a more negative response. Students will be able to write an answer to the question from both viewpoints. This exercise is designed to allow students the opportunity to use their imaginations and, at the same time, think logically and with some concept of responsibility toward actions.

DIRECTIONS:

The following pages can be duplicated for classroom use. Each question has room for two responses. Encourage students to think in a logical fashion. Make sure they understand that if certain actions were to develop from the situation presented, they should be aware of possible consequences that could result.

Name _____

1. What if you won a national sweepstakes that included a trip and lots of money?
(good response)

_____

_____

_____

_____

_____

_____

_____

_____

(bad response)

_____

_____

_____

_____

_____

_____

_____

_____

2. What if your school ordered in pizza each day for lunch?

(good response)

_____

_____

_____

_____

_____

_____

_____

(bad response)

_____

_____

_____

_____

_____

_____

_____

Name _____

3. What if your school had no rules?

(good response)

_____

_____

_____

_____

_____

_____

_____

(bad response)

_____

_____

_____

_____

_____

_____

_____

Name _____

4. What if your community was without electricity for a week?

(good response)

_____

_____

_____

_____

_____

_____

_____

(bad response)

_____

_____

_____

_____

_____

_____

_____

_____

Name _____

5. What if your teacher allowed you to teach class for one day?
(good response)

_____

_____

_____

_____

_____

_____

_____

(bad response)

_____

_____

_____

_____

_____

_____

_____

Name _____

6. What if you were accidentally left behind in a local mall?

(good response)

_____

_____

_____

_____

_____

_____

_____

_____

(bad response)

_____

_____

_____

_____

_____

_____

_____

_____

Name _____

7. What if students were not permitted to speak once they entered the school building?

(good response)

_____

_____

_____

_____

_____

_____

_____

_____

(bad response)

_____

_____

_____

_____

_____

_____

_____

_____

Name _____

8. What if it didn't rain for a full year?

(good response)

_____

_____

_____

_____

_____

_____

_____

(bad response)

_____

_____

_____

_____

_____

_____

_____

Name _____

9. What if you had to attend school six days a week?

or

What if you had to attend school the year round?

(good response)

_____

_____

_____

_____

_____

_____

_____

(bad response)

_____

_____

_____

_____

_____

_____

_____

_____

Creative Writing—What If's

10. What if your school played popular music over the intercom each school day?

(good response)

_____

_____

_____

_____

_____

_____

_____

(bad response)

_____

_____

_____

_____

_____

_____

_____

The WORD Is . . .

W

Organization

R

D

Is . . .

Part II

The Word is...Organization

One extremely important aspect of good writing is organization. Organizational skills begin with organized thinking. The writer who has organizational skills has the ability to know what fits and what does not. Also, the organized writer can effectively combine proper elements and know why that combination works best. This section of the book deals with a variety of organizational skills which can enhance organizational thinking.

The first crucial element of organization is **unity**. The exercise is designed to help develop logical thinking without wandering or getting off track.

The second exercise on organization will help the writer to distinguish between what is **general** and what is **specific**. Also, the exercise will allow the student to see the relationships between the two.

The third organizational skill covered is **classification**. This exercise provides the writer with the challenge of putting ideas and things together and knowing why they fit.

Another important skill of organization is the ability to see differences or **contrast**. Three different exercises are included which will help to develop this skill.

The fifth element of organizational thinking is **logical order**. In this exercise, students will arrange things or ideas in orders that are either logical, natural, or familiar.

The sixth skill of organization is supporting general ideas with **specific examples.** This exercise also provides the teacher with a better understanding of the student's knowledge base. A follow-up exercise will reverse the process and allow students to provide general ideas from specific examples.

The final organizational skill covered is that of recognizing and providing **parts** or specific details to create the **whole**. A follow-up exercise will allow students the opportunity to reverse the process by suggesting a whole made from given parts.

Name _____

UNITY

DIRECTIONS:

In each of the following groups of words, one does not fit. Underline the word that does not belong. On the line below the list of words, explain why that word does not fit. The first one has been done for you .

1. sewing, coin collecting, woodworking, <u>sleeping</u>, stamp collecting
   Sleeping is not a hobby.
   _____

2. soda, milk, kerosene, juice, water, tea
   _____

3. shirt, knife, shoes, pants, socks, cap
   _____

4. trot, gallop, cantor, sprint, run, leap
   _____

5. scream, whisper, holler, yell, shout, screech
   _____

6. car, sofa, bed, chair, footstool, table
   _____

7. hockey, baseball, tennis, anchor, football, track
   _____

8. sleet, rocks, rain, snow, hail, fog
   _____

9. anger, stare, smile, frown, blush, sneer
   _____

10. hammer, screwdriver, wrench, saw, metal, chisel
    _____

11. ice cream, fudge, celery, cookie, cake, pie
    _____

Name _____

GENERAL / SPECIFIC

DIRECTIONS:

In the list of words below, circle the one word that actually includes all the others and could be a title for them.

1. tinsel, lights, wreath, decorations, ribbons, balls

2. weather, humidity, winds, temperature, rain, fog

3. dog, hamster, parakeet, cat, pet, rabbit

4. ant, fly, gnat, grasshopper, mosquito, insect

5. maple, tree, willow, oak, pine, cedar

6. corn, beans, peas, carrots, vegetables, lettuce

7. piano, instrument, drum, trumpet, violin, flute

8. rose, violet, daisy, flower, lily, mum

9. fruit, apple, peach, banana, orange, pear

10. cardinal, crow, bird, sparrow, bluejay, wren

11. games, dolls, puzzles, stuffed animals, toys, models

12. carpenter, worker, plumber, electrician, bricklayer, mechanic

Name _____

CLASSIFICATION

DIRECTIONS:

The following groups contain six words which can be put into two subgroups of three words each. Write on the lines provided 1) the main heading for both groups, 2) the subgroup heading, and 3) the items for each subgroup. The first one has been done for you.

1. ITEMS: wool silk orlon polyester nylon cotton

MAIN HEADING Fabrics_____

SUBHEADING Natural_____   SUBHEADING Man-made_____

a. wool_____   a. nylon_____

b. silk_____   b. orlon_____

c. cotton_____   c. polyester_____

2. ITEMS: beef carrots pork potatoes spinach veal

MAIN HEADING_____

SUBHEADING _____   SUBHEADING _____

a. _____   a. _____

b. _____   b. _____

c. _____   c. _____

3. ITEMS: sheep wolves goats deer cows lions

MAIN HEADING _____

SUBHEADING _____   SUBHEADING _____

a. _____   a. _____

b. _____   b. _____

c. _____   c. _____

4. ITEMS: soccer baseball swimming golf football skiing

MAIN HEADING _____

SUBHEADING _____   SUBHEADING _____

a. _____   a. _____

b. _____   b. _____

c. _____   c. _____

5. ITEMS: cap boots hat shoes slippers turban

MAIN HEADING _____

SUBHEADING _____   SUBHEADING _____

a. _____   a. _____

b. _____   b. _____

c. _____   c. _____

Name _____

CONTRAST

DIRECTIONS FOR EXERCISE 1:

From the pool of words below, select the one that is the opposite of the words which are numbered, and write the word on the line.

stretch	start	sell	lose
happy	float	failure	create

1. success _____

2. sink _____

3. sad _____

4. finish _____

5. find _____

6. destroy _____

7. buy _____

8. shrink _____

DIRECTIONS FOR EXERCISE 2:

In each of the groups containing four words, circle the two words that are opposites.

1. awkward graceful funny slim

2. soft dark hard rich

3. known poor forgotten slow

4. follow lead jump say

5. horn safety danger basket

6. tiny always old never

7. ask break repair try

8. ancient tired sad modern

9. friend pet hero coward

10. late seldom always when

Name _____

DIRECTIONS FOR EXERCISE 3:

For the words listed below, write as many opposites as you can.

1. over _____

2. champion _____

3. large _____

4. none _____

5. close _____

6. fast _____

7. walk _____

8. sad _____

9. new _____

10. loud _____

11. dark _____

12. enemy _____

13. thin _____

14. empty _____

15. end _____

16. straight _____

17. dull _____

18. release _____

19. smooth _____

20. open _____

Name _____

LOGICAL ORDER

DIRECTIONS:

Use the space to the right to arrange the words in some order that makes sense to you. The first one has been done for you.

1. aim
   fire
   ready

   ready, aim, fire _____

2. animal
   boxer
   dog
   mammal

   _____

3. breeze
   calm
   tornado
   wind

   _____

4. average
   large
   huge
   enormous

   _____

5. ocean
   puddle
   lake
   pond

   _____

6. walk
   jog
   sprint
   crawl

   _____

7. wall
   floor
   ceiling

   _____

Name _____

SPECIFIC EXAMPLES

DIRECTIONS FOR EXERCISE 1:

For each general idea you are given one example. You are to add two more specific examples of your own.

1. Things seen on a highway
   cars
   _____   _____

2. Great sports figures
   Babe Ruth
   _____   _____

3. Healthful foods
   fruit
   _____   _____

4. Common tools
   hammer
   _____   _____

5. Friendly dogs
   collie
   _____   _____

6. Zoo animals
   elephant
   _____   _____

7. Types of automobiles
   station wagon
   _____   _____

8. Common jobs
   Teaching
   _____   _____

9. Clothing
   scarf
   _____   _____

Name _____

MORE SPECIFIC EXAMPLES

DIRECTIONS FOR EXERCISE 2:

In this exercise you are given only the general idea. You must supply all three specific examples.

1. Major rivers of the world

   _____   _____   _____

2. Common diseases

   _____   _____   _____

3. Great inventions

   _____   _____   _____

4. Boring chores

   _____   _____   _____

5. Things that use a rope

   _____   _____   _____

6. Things used to set a dinner table

   _____   _____   _____

7. Great scientists

   _____   _____   _____

Name _____

CREATING GENERAL IDEAS

DIRECTIONS:

You have already worked at developing specific examples from a general idea. Now you are asked to write a general idea from a list of specific examples. The first one is done for you.

1. vanilla, chocolate, Neapolitan, fudge marble _____ice cream_____

2. earthquakes, floods, tornadoes, hurricanes _____

3. Alexander, Caesar, Napoleon, Hitler _____

4. Hindu, Islam, Christianity _____

5. stars, moon, sun, meteorites _____

6. hands, feet, face, elbows, knees _____

7. hands, face, numbers, crystal _____

8. fried, scrambled, soft, hard _____

9. Cy Young, Warren Spahn, Bob Gibson, Tom Seaver _____

10. backstroke, butterfly, freestyle, breaststroke _____

11. army, air force, navy, marines _____

12. cheddar, Roquefort, Swiss, cottage _____

13. Susan B. Anthony, Coretta King, Madam Curie _____

14. spears, crossbows, swords, catapults _____

15. snake, alligator, crocodile, tortoise _____

16. triangle, square, rectangle, circle _____

17. lipstick, powder, rouge, eyeliner _____

Name _____

PARTS OF A WHOLE

DIRECTIONS:

In each of the following, you are given a whole and two of its parts. You are to supply two more parts of the same whole. The first one is done for you.

1. a person's face

   nose   eyes   _____mouth_____   _____chin_____

2. a kitchen

   cabinets stove   _____   _____

3. library

   books   magazines   _____   _____

4. baseball diamond

   mound   bases   _____   _____

In the following, you are only given the whole. You must supply the four parts.

1. an ear of corn

   _____ _____ _____ _____

2. fishing tackle

   _____ _____ _____ _____

3. a beach

   _____ _____ _____ _____

Name _____

FROM PARTS TO THE WHOLE

DIRECTIONS:

In this exercise you must determine the whole from the list of parts given.

1. mats, ropes, floor, parallel bars _____

2. courts, president, congress, cabinet _____

3. bumper, fender, windshield, tires _____

4. beds, doctors, nurses, medicine _____

5. speaker, turntable, decks, tuner _____

6. bulb, base, switch, shade _____

7. petal, stem, root, pollen _____

8. mouth, bank, source, bed _____

9. stage, seats, curtain, screen _____

10. briefcase, suit, car-phone _____

11. paper, ribbon, bow, tag _____

12. water, filter, gravel, light _____

13. blade, wheel, rope, handle _____

The

W
O
Research
D

Is . . .

Part III

73

The Word is . . .Research

The scavenger hunt activities that follow are designed to encourage students to use reference works and other sources to find out answers. You can structure these activities however you wish. They might be done just for enjoyment or as a game between teams. They could be used and graded as part of a unit on the library or research.

The scavenger hunts cover the areas of American History, the American Civil War, people, places and things. Activities are included at two different levels of difficulty.

We have found that it works best to set a time limit and award prizes to the student(s) that find the most answers.

Other activities included under the heading of Research are Dictionary Fun, Rocket Launch, Interview, Storytelling, and a lengthy section on Heroes.

If your students are not familiar with reference works, you will need to preface these activities with minimal teaching about what is in each source and how to use them. However, these activities are intended to develop students' awareness of what the sources contain. With many classes it may be possible or best to let them begin research activities by looking for answers by trial and error in the different sources.

74

Scavenger Hunt

A scavenger hunt is where you look for unusual, lost, or unknown things. Today, you are going on a scavenger hunt in the library. Your mission? To look for the unusual, lost, and unknown answers to the questions below. Only the general category has been given to you. Use your knowledge of encyclopedias, almanacs, dictionaries, books, and reference works to find the answers.

American Civil War

1) Who was the main or keynote speaker when the Gettysburg Address was delivered?

2) What famous decoration, the highest awarded a U.S. serviceman, was created by Congress in 1861?

3) What two new states were admitted to the Union on June 20, 1863, and on October 31, 1864?

4) What was Ulysses S. Grant's real given name?

5) On what was Harriet Tubman's fame based?

6) What organization did Clara Barton help to start?

7) On what date did Vicksburg, Mississippi, surrender to Union forces, and who was the Union's commanding general?

8) What were the "Quaker guns" used at times by Confederate forces?

9) What general marched to the sea declaring, "War is cruelty. There is no use trying to reform it. The crueler it is, the sooner it will be over."?

10) What were the "butternuts" commonly worn by Confederates? How did they get this nickname?

Scavenger Hunt

A scavenger hunt is where you look for unusual, lost, or unknown things. Today, you are going on a scavenger hunt in the library. Your mission? To look for the unusual, lost, and unknown answers to the questions below. Only the general category has been given to you. Use your knowledge of encyclopedias, almanacs, dictionaries, books, and reference works to find the answers.

American History

1) Who was Jane Addams and why was she famous?

2) What were three tribes that belonged to the Iroquois Confederation?

3) What famous American landmark is located in the Black Hills of South Dakota?

4) Who won the Indy 500 in 1990 and 1991?

5) What is an incumbent?

6) When did Charles Lindbergh fly across the Atlantic? Why did it make him famous?

7) To what tribe did the war chief Crazy Horse belong?

8) When was Frederick Douglass born? When did he die?

9) Who were the Presidents during the 1920's?

10) What slogan appears on American currency?

11) When did Amelia Earhart disappear?

12) In what year did Hawaii become a state?

Name _____

Scavenger Hunt

Have you ever been on a scavenger hunt? The object of this game is to find out who the mystery person, place, or thing is by using reference materials in the library. The clues below refer to ten famous <u>people</u>. Put your answer in the blank under each set of clues.

1) Home run leader before Aaron
    "Sultan of Swat"
    Played in Boston first

    _____

2) Jelly bean lover, no peanuts
    "The Gipper"
    Oldest President

    _____

3) "Air" man
    North Carolina man
    Bullish roundball man

    _____

4) Wife of famous razorback
    Lawyer
    First Lady

    _____

5) King Arthur's lady
    Queen for more than a day
    Camelot her home

    _____

6) Ran for Vice President
    Mondale's helper in 1976
    First woman to do so

    _____

7) Razorback
    Gore's buddy
    Commander-in-chief

    _____

8) "Great Emancipator"
    16th President
    "Railsplitter"

    _____

9) Red Cross founder
    Nurse
    Civil War lady

    _____

10) "Moses" of Underground
    Helped slaves to freedom
    "Northern Star"

    _____

Name _____

Scavenger Hunt

*Have you ever been on a scavenger hunt? The object of this game is to find out who the mystery person, place, or thing is by using reference materials in the library. The clues below refer to ten famous <u>places</u>. Put your answer in the blank under each set of clues.

1) Torch of freedom
    New York harbor
    Welcomes immigrants

    _____

2) Colorado river at bottom
    In Nevada
    Colorful, deep hole

    _____

3) Big Ben here
    Thames city
    Shakespeare played here

    _____

4) Arctic Zone
    Farthest north
    90 degrees N

    _____

5) Earthquake state
    L.A., San Francisco
    Golden Bear

    _____

6) Not in a state
    Many monuments here
    Presidents live here

    _____

7) Eiffel Tower
    Arc de Triomphe
    Seine River

    _____

8) Oil wells here
    Near Red Sea
    Mostly desert

    _____

9) Northern U.S. neighbor
    Ottawa capital
    Big hockey fans

    _____

10) Crescent City
    Superdome there
    Mardi Gras

    _____

Name _____

Scavenger Hunt

*Have you ever been on a scavenger hunt? The object of this game is to find out who the mystery person, place, or thing is by using reference materials in the library. The clues below refer to ten famous <u>things</u>. Put your answer in the blank under each set of clues.

1) Inuit use as homes
    Ice blocks
    Found in Arctic

    _____

2) Astronauts ride it
    Can be reused
    Atlantis one

    _____

3) Arms and legs a part
    Sternum in middle
    Skeleton inside

    _____

4) Humpback
    Air breathing swimmer
    Biggest mammal

    _____

5) Hot stuff
    Radiation does job
    Popcorn popper

    _____

6) Buffalo hide house
    Portable homes
    Native American house

    _____

7) Iris
    Vision leader
    Different pupil

    _____

8) Elephant teeth
    Ivory
    Found in Africa

    _____

9) Ash is its wood
    3 swings and it's out
    Some aluminum

    _____

10) Last
    Sole pair
    Comes in all sizes

    _____

Library Scavenger Hunt Answer Key

American Civil War

1. Edward Everett
2. The Congressional Medal of Honor
3. West Virginia, Nevada
4. Hiram Ulysses Grant
5. She led slaves over the Underground Railroad
6. American Red Cross
7. July 4, 1863; U.S. Grant
8. Logs painted black to look like cannon
9. William T. Sherman
10. Brownish uniforms. Butternuts or oak bark were crushed to make the dye for them.

American History

1. She was the founder of Hull House in Chicago, and she worked to help improve the lives of poor families.
2. Seneca, Onondaga, Oneida, Mohawk, Cayuga
3. Mt. Rushmore
4. 1990: Arie Luyendyk; 1991: Rick Mears
5. An office holder running for reelection.
6. 1927. He flew alone.
7. Sioux
8. Born: 1817; Died: 1895
9. Wilson, Coolidge, Hoover
10. In God We Trust
11. Disappeared on around-the-world flight in 1937
12. 1959

People

1. Babe Ruth
2. Ronald Reagan
3. Michael Jordan
4. Hillary Clinton
5. Guenievere
6. Geraldine Ferraro
7. Bill Clinton
8. Abraham Lincoln
9. Clara Barton
10. Harriet Tubman

Places

1. Statue of Liberty
2. Grand Canyon
3. London
4. Arctic
5. California
6. Washington, D.C.
7. Paris
8. Saudi Arabia
9. Canada
10. New Orleans

Things

1. igloo
2. space shuttle
3. human body
4. whale
5. microwave oven
6. tepee
7. eye
8. elephant tusk
9. baseball bat
10. shoe

Dictionary Fun

Did you know that you can be found in a dictionary? Well, you can. To prove this, look in a dictionary and find two words that describe your personality. But, the words must begin with your first initial and your last initial ! Here's an example:

Sarah Peters

_ _ _ _ r
_ _ _ e
_ _ t
y _ t
_ _ y

Put the letters of your name below, and see how many words you can find that describe your personality and begin with your first initial and last initial. For more fun, you can also find words that match the rest of the letters in your name!

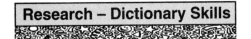

Rocket Launch

This is a game intended to improve students' dictionary skills. It takes place in two stages. In the first stage, students look up an assigned list of 15 to 20 words. As they find the meaning of each one, they write it down on a 3 x 5 card and bring the card up to their team's launching pad diagram (see outline drawing) that is taped on the board. The first team to build its launching pad in this way gets 10 points, the second 9, etc. The team with the most points at the end of the game gets a prize/grade points, second place a smaller prize/fewer grade points, etc.

Once the teams have finished building their launching pads, the teacher records the scores and tapes the rocket ship diagram to the board above the top of the launching pad. The rocket ship (see outline drawing) is composed of two stages and a space shuttle. The teacher announces that tomorrow the class will play a rocket launch game, and that everyone should study the words that they have looked up in class as homework tonight.

In the second part of this game, the students are quizzed on the meanings of the words they looked up yesterday. If they think that they know a word (as the teacher says the meaning of a word aloud), they can put the 3 x 5 card for that word on a part of the rocket or space shuttle as they sit together ready for launching. When a team has the whole rocket and shuttle filled in (10-12 spaces: see outline drawing), it can shout "Lift off!" and jump up in the air. If they have any incorrect words, the team's launch will "abort," and that team gets 0 points at the end. Since all teams can theoretically "lift off" at the same time, all teams that correctly put up all ten words receive the same points.

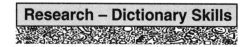

Launching Pad

Your teacher will show you how to draw this and the space shuttle on the board, or how to use an overhead projector to enlarge and trace the diagrams to make them bigger!

			Put
			Word Cards
			Here

Put
1
Word Card
Here

Put
1
Word Card
Here

Put
1
Word Card
Here

83

Space
Shuttle

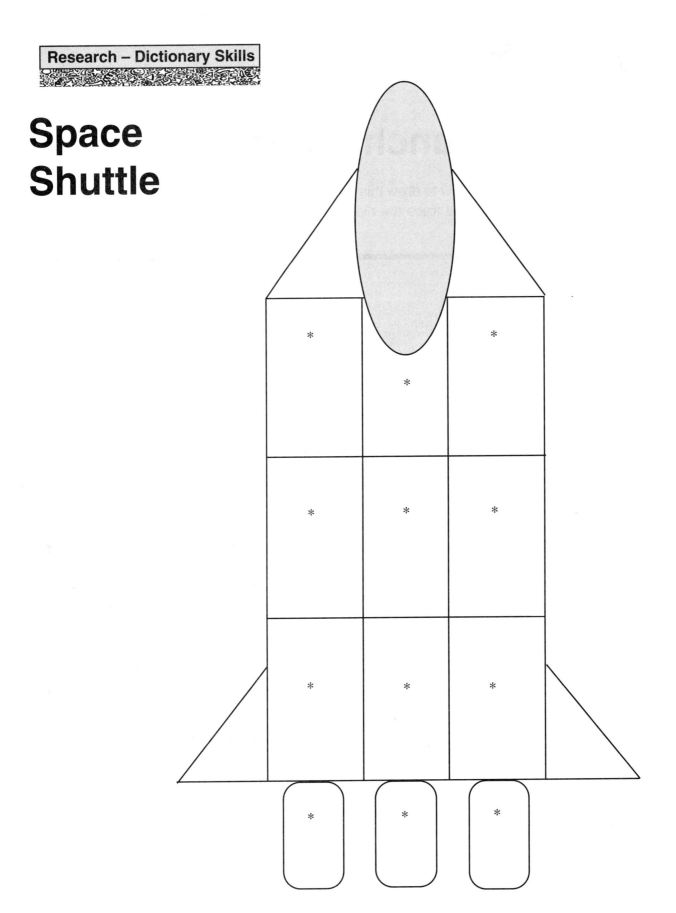

Put one word card on each space with a * in it

84

Interview

An interview is a time for asking someone questions. These questions can be about a person's life, job, family, friends, future plans, or any number of other things.

Interviews are used by reporters for newspapers and television stations. They should describe someone and give some information about that person that will paint a word picture of him or her.

You are going to interview someone in class and then do a biography of that person.

Here are some sample questions to use. Bet you can think up even more and better ones to ask! Write the answers down on a sheet of paper.

-What is your age, weight, height, sex?

-Where do you live?

-How long have you lived in our town/city?

-Do you have any relatives that live here? Where do all of your relatives live?

-How far back can your family trace your ancestors? From where did they come?

-What do your parents do for a living?

-How many people are in your family?

-What is your favorite music? Group?

-Do you have any hobbies?

-What is your favorite TV show?

-What is your favorite book?

-What is your favorite sport? Do you have a favorite sports star?

-What types of clothes do you like to wear? Why?

-What are your plans for the future?

Storytelling

What's your favorite story that your grandparents tell? Is it funny, scary, or just cool?

This project is to retell your favorite story told to you by your grandparents. You can retell this story to the class out loud, or write it out.

To help you remember the story, talk to your grandparents and ask them to tell you the story again. Take notes below, paying special attention to the names of the people in the story, the order in which things take place, and how the story begins and ends.

Beginning of story

Names of people/characters

Order of events

End of story

Heroes

Hero-worship has existed and will always exist among young people. The problem seems to be the rapidly changing character of the hero. Some people would certainly question the definition of today's hero as compared to that of past heroes. Former U.S. Secretary of State Henry Kissinger once said: "I think any society needs individuals that symbolize what it stands for." Yet, some psychologists today feel that heroes are a thing of the past.

What makes a hero? Do we need them? The next several pages are devoted to heroes past and present, from the superhero to the everyday hero. Students will be given the opportunity to write about different types of heroes, using their own knowledge as well as research.

One definition of a hero states that the person must be noble, have high aims or goals, and possess the courage to see those goals accomplished. You may have a definition of your own. The hero section of this book will present five types of heroes: the historical, the legendary, the superhero, the contemporary or modern, and the everyday or unsung. Students can write about any or all types of heroes using their own background and knowledge. Some students may like the challenge of researching the historical or legendary hero before they write. Either way, you will want students to express their reasons for identifying the person as a hero. You may ask that the students relate their findings to the definition given above or to a definition of your own.

You might begin the writing project by first discussing heroes. You can ask students to name individuals they feel are their heroes. Then have them discuss the physical and moral qualities that the person possesses. This type of pre-writing activity can be done in large or small group situations. This writing project can ultimately lead to an oral presentation for some students.

HISTORICAL HERO - Students are to research a famous person. Questions are provided that are applicable to all heroes. A page of names is also included for duplication and distribution. You will also find some blank boxes for your own or your students' own entries.

LEGENDARY HERO - You may seek the help of your librarian in pulling possible materials for this category. Once again, a set of questions and a page of names are available, along with blank boxes for your own contributions.

SUPERHERO - This category grows and grows with each generation. The list of names is in no way exhaustive. Your students will probably be very capable of adding the names of the latest and greatest superheroes. Space has been provided for all additions, and a page of pertinent questions can be duplicated for easy use. Students can also add a picture or drawing of the hero.

MODERN HERO - This category will probably include many of the names students provided in the pre-writing discussion session. This category will include names of celebrities, from sports stars to film and music stars. This exercise simply asks students to write why they selected that particular person as their hero and provide a picture.

EVERYDAY HERO - Using newspaper and magazine articles, students can find pictures and write about the heroic efforts of common citizens who seldom become famous, but who exhibit the qualities of "true heroes" in our society.

Name _____

THE HISTORICAL HERO

1. What is the name of your hero? _____

2. List the kind of deeds that made the person famous.

   _____

   _____

   _____

   _____

   _____

   _____

   _____

3. What specific qualities (physical or moral) did this person have in order to do what he or she did?

   _____

   _____

   _____

4. What effect did the deeds of this person have on society then?

   _____

   _____

   _____

5. Are we still affected today by the deeds of this hero? How?

   _____

   _____

6. What sources did you use for your information?

   _____

Name _____

THE HISTORICAL HERO

_____

_____

_____

_____

_____

_____

_____

_____

_____

_____

_____

_____

_____

_____

THOMAS JEFFERSON	WINSTON CHURCHILL
JOAN OF ARC	GEORGE WASHINGTON CARVER
THOMAS EDISON	FLORENCE NIGHTINGALE
HARRIET TUBMAN	SERGEANT ALVIN YORK

MADAM CURIE	AMELIA EARHART
BENJAMIN FRANKLIN	MARTIN LUTHER KING, JR.
CHARLES LINDBERGH	AUDIE MURPHY
GENERAL GEORGE PATTON	FREDERICK DOUGLASS

JIM BOWIE	CHIEF JOSEPH
WRIGHT BROTHERS	MALCOM X
JOHN KENNEDY	JESSE OWENS
GHANDHI	RED CLOUD

Name _____

THE LEGENDARY HERO

1. Who is your legendary hero? _____

2. Was your hero a real person, an imaginary person, or some combination of the two?

   _____

   _____

   _____

   _____

3. What outstanding physical or moral qualities did this person have that allowed him/her to do the great things that made him/her famous?

   _____

   _____

   _____

   _____

   _____

4. Against whom or what did this hero have to struggle?

   _____

   _____

   _____

   _____

5. What did this person do to become a hero? What were some of his/her great feats?

   _____

   _____

   _____

   _____

6. What sources did you use for your information?

   _____

   _____

   _____

Name _____

THE LEGENDARY HERO

_____

_____

_____

_____

_____

_____

_____

_____

_____

_____

_____

_____

_____

_____

_____

PAUL BUNYAN	ROBIN HOOD
ULYSSES	KING ARTHUR
CALAMITY JANE	CASEY JONES
DANIEL BOONE	JOHNNY APPLESEED

HERCULES	JESSE JAMES
PECOS BILL	JOHN HENRY
ANNIE OAKLEY	CHARLEMAGNE
DAVY CROCKETT	ZORRO

Name _____

THE SUPERHERO

picture or drawing

1. Who is your superhero? _____

2. What physical or moral qualities does this hero have?

_____

_____

_____

3. With whom or what does your hero struggle?

_____

_____

_____

4. What special powers, abilities, or tricks does this superhero use?

_____

_____

_____

_____

_____

_____

Name _____

THE SUPERHERO

_____

_____

_____

_____

_____

_____

_____

_____

_____

_____

_____

_____

_____

_____

GAMBIT	SUPERMAN
BATMAN	IRON MAN
CABLE	THE FLASH
CYCLOPS	SPAWN

THE PUNISHER	WONDER WOMAN
INCREDIBLE HULK	SAVAGE DRAGON
GHOST RIDER	SHADOWHAWK
WOLVERINE	CAPTAIN AMERICA

Name _____

THE MODERN HERO

```
┌──────────────────────────────────┐
│                                  │
│                                  │
│                                  │
│                                  │
│                                  │
│                                  │
│                                  │
└──────────────────────────────────┘
```

Picture or drawing

1. Who is your hero today? _____

2. What is your hero known for? What does he or she do in life?

   _____

   _____

   _____

   _____

3. What special qualities does your hero have?

   _____

   _____

   _____

   _____

4. Write a paper that explains why you believe that this person is a hero to you.

103

Name _____

THE MODERN HERO

_____

_____

_____

_____

_____

_____

_____

_____

_____

_____

_____

_____

_____

Name _____

THE EVERYDAY HERO

Picture

Everyday heroes are the people who are not always well-known, but at some time in their lives risk all that they have for someone else. These people might have jobs which put them in such a position every day. Yet, the everyday hero could be someone who happens to be in the right spot at the right time just once in his or her life. This person could be anyone in the community.

Using a newspaper or magazine, find a picture and story of someone who became a hero. In your own words, describe what the person did and what qualities the person displayed while doing the heroic deed. Remember to include how the action of this person fits that of a hero.

Name _____

THE EVERYDAY HERO

_____

_____

_____

_____

_____

_____

_____

_____

_____

_____

_____

_____

The

W

O

R

Doing it all

Is . . .

Part IV

Illumination

One of the best ways to add to a story is by including illustrations (pictures or drawings) with it. In the days before printing presses, monks or scribes used to copy books by hand. To make the books more beautiful, they would add pictures to go with the story. This process of illustration was called "illumination."

On the sheet given you by your teacher, copy down your favorite story line-by-line. Put your story's title first on the line at the top of the page. Then, put a ruler underneath each line as you write it, or put a piece of lined notebook paper behind the page you are writing on and use the lines that show through as guides to keep your writing straight. Finally, add a drawing to your story in the box on the left hand side.

Your drawing or illumination can be about anything, as long as it is related to the story in some way. The more interesting and colorful the illumination, the better the story will be.

Name _____

Library Design

Your students will probably use the library/media center at your school for many things. At a minimum, they should be familiar enough with the room to be able to find books or other materials. This exercise aims to help them become aware of the layout of the library/media center room, and to extend their creativity to think about how that area could be improved and made even more effective.

Students should be as precise as possible in developing the layout of the actual room and in creating the theoretical "better" room. This activity aims to teach students organization skills, preciseness, a sense of space, and a sense of priority in making choices.

This activity can also be done as a cooperative project with students that are better at figures doing the computing and drawing, and students that are not so strong in these areas doing the measurement. Other than the sheets provided, the students will need only pencil, tape or glue, a measuring device (tape measures work best), and access to the library/media center. Graph paper may help them draw to scale, but it is not strictly necessary since scale drawings can be made using only a ruler. We recommend a scale of 1 inch = 3 feet. This is small enough to show detail, yet not so small as to make drawing a large room difficult. If students use graph paper, they can draw at the scale of 1 square = 1 foot.

You will know best whether to organize your students by individuals or teams. After the original measuring and map making of the actual media center/library, encourage students to brainstorm the thing(s) needed to improve the media center/library and make it more beneficial for students. They then can prioritize this list to create their ideal media center/library. For advanced/gifted students you can even give them a budget and do cost estimates for the improvements. Improvements can include greater space for the media center/library.

All students should use the same symbols for furniture, and other items to include in their designs. If they do not do so, there is no common language for them to compare their designs with each other.

Name _____

Library Design

Today everyone will take on the role of architect. Your school has hired you because you are well-known for the quality of your work. You are to draw a map of your school's library/media center that shows all of the main features of it (furniture, book cases, tables, computers, check out area, doors, windows, etc.). You must draw this map as an overhead view and to scale. To scale means that **one inch on the map below equals three feet** in the actual library/media center.

To draw your map you must do several things carefully:

  -1)measure the dimensions of the room

  -2)measure the sizes of all of the major objects in the room

  -3)accurately place the objects on your map by drawing them

      to scale <u>where they belong</u>

  -4)include doors, windows and other features

Drawing doors and windows for an overhead view is easy if you use these symbols:

DOOR   WINDOW

The most important thing to do is to measure accurately! Then get a specific idea of how things are arranged in the room.

Use a piece of typing paper or graph paper to draw a to-scale drawing of the outside dimensions of the room. It might look like this:

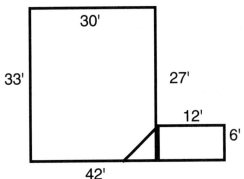

Notice how this room is sized. The closet/storage room or office on the right is 6 feet wide at the door and 12 feet long. The main part of the library/media center is 30 feet wide and 33 feet long. There are no windows in this room. Now architect, get to work on your measurements of your library/ media center!

112

Name _____

Library Design

Now that your architectural firm has made measurements of the actual library/media center, you have been hired to develop a design for a new and improved library/media center. To make improvements you must have a good idea of the changes or additions that need to be made in the current library/media center. These changes or additions can include anything like more space, computers, more book shelves, reading areas with comfortable chairs, TV/VCR areas. Let your imagination run wild; but after you have made your list, you should rank the changes/additions from most to least needed.

Brainstorm A List of Changes/Additions for the Library

_____

_____

_____

_____

_____

_____

_____

_____

_____

WRITE DOWN AS MANY IDEAS AS YOU CAN THINK OF ! ! !

Name _____

Design for the New Library/Media Center

Draw your design for the new, improved library/media center below. You can use any shape that you want, but you should tape or glue down the symbols for bookcases, tables, etc. that your teacher will give you. Remember to draw/design to scale ! Don't forget to include at least one door!

114

Symbols to Use for the New Library

BOOKCASE   **SMALL STAND/CASE**   **TABLES**

CHAIRS   **COMPUTERS**   **SHELVES**

TV/VCR   **CARD CATALOG**   **FILE CABINETS**

CHECK-OUT DESK

SCALE FOR THESE SYMBOLS IS 1" = 3 '

115

Doing It All – Library Design

Name _____

Why Our New Library Design Is Better

You will have to tell the class why you put the things you did in your new library design. Think about your choices, and write your reasons for putting in the things you did below. Then you can read these reasons to the class when you show them your design. Remember to write down a reason for each thing that you put in your design. Don't forget anything !

_____

_____

_____

_____

_____

_____

_____

_____

_____

_____

_____

_____

_____

_____

_____

_____

_____

_____

Scriptwriting

This activity will allow your students to engage in several writing activities and integrate them into a film that they will write, direct, film, and act in.

Students should first draw up skeleton outlines of the plots of their stories. They will then discuss and review technical movie language.

Incorporating this background information on plot and technical language, the students will write rough "shooting scripts." Polishing these scripts, students will revise them and then "hire" actors (classmates) to be in the films.

The activity has closure in students acting in and filming all scripts, or at least a part of each one. This can be done by using a school's camcorder.

Activity worksheets are provided to help you talk your students through all the steps of writing and making a movie. Acting in and filming the movie replaces the normal publication step used with student writing.

You could also use the technical talk terms for a vocabulary quiz, or spin-off other activities from the screenplay.

Scriptwriting

Ever wanted to make your own movie? Well, here is your chance to write a script (story) for your own movie. A script is written like a play, but includes even more descriptions of what is happening to tell exactly what is seen by the camera's "eye."

Scriptwriter _____

Write down a skeleton outline of the plot of your story below. This need not have much detail. You will use it mainly to get your events in correct order.

    Example: -1)Bloody hand is seen

                  -2)Scream is heard

                  -3)Woman is seen running away

Now, begin your own script with a skeleton outline.

-1)

-2)

-3)

-4)

-5)

-6)

Scriptwriting

Movie "Technical Talk"

Movie makers use a lot of technical words to describe what the camera sees. This is especially true for the camera's point of view.

Technical talk terms

Normal view	looking into the eyes of an actor who is speaking
Reverse view	looking over the shoulder of an actor who is speaking
High angle	the camera looks down on the actors from above their eye level
Normal angle	the camera looks at the actors' eye level
Low angle	the camera looks at the actors from below eye level
Long shot	frames a whole room or field
Medium shot	frames a subject's body from head to feet
Close-up shot	frames a part of something, like a subject's head and shoulders
Extreme close-up	frames a small part of something, like only a subject's eyes

*All of these terms can be written in shorthand.

NVNAMS = normal view, normal angle, medium shot

The shorthand (abbreviation) above is called a shot selection or shot.

Scriptwriting

Other terms used in movie technical talk:

zoom   to change shots from long to medium (zoom in), or
                  close-up to long (zoom out)

pan   to turn the camera from side-to-side, but to keep it
                  still. Like a person seated at a tennis match watching the action.

dolly   to move the camera along a certain route

cut   to move quickly (cut) from one shot to another

dissolve   a shot that fades away

lap dissolve a shot that fades away and, as it does, is slowly replaced by
                  another shot

fade-to-black a shot fades away to a black screen

Name _____

Scriptwriting

*Look at the shots below and identify each one as either a long shot (LS), medium shot (MS), close-up (CS), or extreme close-up (ECU).

-1)

_____

-2)

_____

-3)

_____

-4)

_____

Name _____

Scriptwriting

*Use your skeleton outline to write a shooting script. The example below will show you how to provide all of the details.

Example: 3 second shot   NVHAECU of a bloody hand sticking out from under a bed

2 second shot   RVNAMS of a woman as she walks into the bed room

2 second shot   NVNACU woman screams, "Oh, no !"

(The 3 shots above would be 7 seconds of filming in a movie.)

Sportswriting

This activity uses sports statistics to encourage students to organize information and be creative. Although this activity focuses on sports, there is no reason that other areas of human activity, such as dance, music, or film, might not be used in this way to do a similar activity. Creative students may even wish to substitute information about people in one of these other areas for the sports information given. This should work well as long as the basic learning design is preserved: to require students to organize facts into a lively recreation.

In this activity, students will use season and game statistics to write a "game report." This report can take the form of a newspaper story or a radio or television sports segment.

The names given in the statistics lists for each "game" are not necessarily the ones students must or will use in their writing. However, they should stick to the same statistics. By doing this, a basis of comparison will be established. If everyone uses his creativity to develop a "game report" story from the same statistics, grading by the teacher will be easier and student interest higher.

Lengths of "game reports" can be altered. A one page written report or a one minute long radio/ TV presentation is suggested. Students may wish to work cooperatively and do more than one "game report" of two different sports.

Name _____

Sportswriting

(Newspaper)

Look over the statistics and game summary page carefully. Then, write a newspaper story on the game and the two teams. Begin below with a lead, or first paragraph, that says the final score, who won, and the team's streaks.

Lead Paragraph

Name _____

Sportswriting

(Radio)

Look over the statistics for the game and season for each team carefully. Then write a radio sports report on the game and the two teams. Put as much detail into your report as you can, since those who are listening did not see the game and are depending on you to tell them what happened. Your report should be about 1 minute long. You should be prepared to give this report to class "over the air" by tomorrow!

Sportswriting. . .Football

Ever wanted to be a sportswriter or a radio or television sports reporter? Well, here is your chance! Below you will see a set of season statistics for a pair of football teams, and a set of "facts" from a game between the same two teams. Your job is to use the season statistics and the game facts to write a story about the game and season for these two teams. Look over the facts, and then write your story on the form sheet.

MADISON MAULERS

Rushing   27—132 yds.

Passing   21-33—243 yds. 2 INT.

Fields Goals 3 for 4 from 33, 36, 45 yds.

Sacks allowed   5 for -54 yds.

Punts   6 for 48.7 yd. avg.

Individuals:

RUSHING: R. Jones 18-123, J. Wyoming 9-9; **PASSING:** J. Wyoming 21-33--243 yds., 2 INT. **REC.:** S. Hands 9--189, A. Catch 7--48, Jones 5--6; **SCORING:** TD's Jones 1 (1st), N.T. Lane 1 (3rd: Catch), H.C. Andersen 3 FG's, 2 PAT's

WHITE BAY GULLS

Rushing 33—193

Passing 17-21—189 yds. 0 INT.

Field Goals   2 for 4 from 51, 54 yds.

Sacks allowed   1 for -6 yds.

Punts   3 for 54.3 yd. avg.

Individuals:

RUSHING: W. Payless 24-123, C. Okguy 9-70; **PASSING:** J. Heisman 17-21--189 yds. 0 INT. **SCORING:** TD's Payless 1; **REC.:** T. Bambi, 10--102, D. Dropit 7--87; **SCORING:** Payless (1st), Okguy 2 (3rd, 4th), M. Longrange 2 FG's, 3 PAT's

SCORING BY QUARTERS

	1	2	3	4	FINAL
MAULERS	10	0	10	3	23
GULLS	13	0	7	7	27

SEASON RECORDS: Maulers 10-2, Gulls 7-5, Maulers' Jones 1123 yds. rushing on season, and Gulls' Payless 1248 yds. rushing on season. S. Hands 99 catches for 1837 yds. on season, and T. Bambi 102 for 1454 yds. on season.

Sportswriting . . . Baseball

Ever wanted to be a sportswriter or a radio or television sports reporter? Well, here is your chance! Below you will see a set of season statistics for a pair of baseball teams and a set of "facts" from a game between the same two teams. Your job is to use the season statistics and the game facts to write a story about the game and season for these two teams. Look over the facts, and then write your story on the form sheet.

JACKSONVILLE VEECKS

	H	AB	R	RBI
Grisley (CF)	3	5	2	2
Finn (LF)	2	4	3	1
Jackson (RF)	1	3	2	0
McEdward (1B)	4	5	1	4
Hayes (3B)	0	5	0	0
Garcia (2B)	2	5	0	0
Blaser (SS)	3	5	0	0
Wilkines (C)	0	5	0	0
Swinandez (P)	0	5	0	0

Pitching: Swinandez 6 2/3 inn., 9 K's, 3 BB, 5 runs, 3 earned (W, now 12-6); S. Holmes 2 1/3 inn., 3 K's, 0 BB, 0 runs (Save, 18th)

ROODHOUSE NATIVES

	H	AB	R	RBI
Bands (LF)	5	5	3	2
Sandman (2B)	3	4	1	0
Hernandez (1B)	0	4	1	0
Holland (3B)	4	4	0	3
Judge (RF)	0	5	0	0
Skyes (CF)	0	5	0	0
Queen (SS)	0	5	0	0
Dallpounds (C)	0	5	0	0
Maddochs (P)	0	5	0	0

Pitching: Maddochs 4 1/3 inn., 4 K's, 3 BB, 0 runs, earned (L, now 9-9); T. Worewell 4 2/3 inn., 0 runs, 0 earned, 0 K's, 0 BB

GAME SUMMARY: 1st INN.: *Grisley doubles for Veecks, Finn walks, Jackson singles, loading bases. McEdward homers, SCORE 4-0. Hayes, Garcia and Blaser fly out to left. Bands, Sandman reach on errors, and Hernandez singles for Natives, Holland triples them home, SCORE 4-3 VEECKS. Judge, Skyes and Queen strike out.* 3rd INN.: *Garcia and Blaser single, and Grisley doubles them home,* SCORE 6-3 VEECKS. *Finn homers,* SCORE 8-3 VEECKS. 5th INN.: *Sandman homers,* SCORE 8-4 VEECKS. 7th INN.: *Sandman homers,* SCORE 8-5 VEECKS. **TEAM RECORDS:** VEECKS 93-33 (WON 7 IN A ROW), NATIVES 90-36 (WON 7 OF LAST 8).

Sportswriting . . . Basketball

Ever wanted to be a sportswriter or a radio or television sports reporter? Well, here is your chance! Below you will see a set of season statistics for a pair of basketball teams and a set of "facts" from a game between the same two teams. Your job is to use the season statistics and the game facts to write a story about the game and season for these two teams. Look over the facts, and then write your story on the form sheet.

DREAM TEAM

	FG	FT	3 PT	REB	MIN.
Byrd (F)	7/11	9/9	3/5	6	36
Jorden (F)	12/18	6/9	6/6	12	40
K. Jawba (C)	5/9	1/7	3/3	18	31
Slick (G)	8/14	1/4	5/9	0	42
Dribble (G)	1/7	2/4	0/0	4	19
K. Nine (G)	3/6	2/6	0/0	6	29
Matso (C-F)	2/4	0/0	0/0	3	25

GLASS MEN

	FG	FT	3 PT	REB	MIN.
M. Majic (F)	9/14	14/16	3/9	1	42
W. Index (F)	3/9	5/7	0/0	24	39
P. Time (C)	12/18	9/11	0/0	21	37
Vitalees (G)	7/18	12/14	9/11	1	39
B. Hogg (G)	1/5	5/7	1/4	3	42
T. Legs (G)	0/5	5/5	2/2	2	15
M. Mann (C-F)	3/7	1/4	0/0	7	26

SCORING BY QUARTERS

	1	2	3	4	FINAL
DREAM TEAM	47	30	40	30	147
GLASS MEN	36	40	40	50	166

STEALS: Jorden 3, Slick 2, Dribble 1, Nine 1; Vitalees 5, Hogg 2

ASSISTS: Slick 9, Nine 7, Jorden 6, Dribble 1; Hogg 12, Vitalees 10

BLOCKS: Jawba 5, Jorden 2, Matso 1; W. Index 4, Time 4, Mann 2

SEASON RECORDS:

> **DREAM TEAM** 42-18 (WON 9 OF 10)

> **GLASS MEN** 41-19 (WON 5 IN A ROW)

INJURIES: Jorden, broken ankle (4th quarter), out 4-6 weeks

WRITING FROM A SPORTSCARD

Homer Trott outfield
Phoenix Mitts

YR	CLUB	G	AB	R	H	2B	3B	HR	RBI	SB	SO	AVG
89	Dogs	16	67	6	9	2	0	1	5	1	10	.134
90	Dogs	97	218	56	97	15	6	12	54	10	65	.444
91	Mitts	155	584	77	152	24	2	43	109	25	143	.260

Homer was a first-round draft pick by the Mitts in 1988 before being sent to Pitchersville to play for the Dogs.
HT: 6'3" WT: 165 BATS: right THROWS: left BORN: 5-8-69

DIRECTIONS: Use the example baseball card above to write the brief baseball history of Homer Trott. Use the information on the card to inform the reader of his career from its start to the year of the card. Write it as a story, adding your own comments about what the player did and what he might do in the future. Remember to use descriptive words to show– not simply tell (example: He has power; He has little speed).

Once you have the task finished, try some on your own by using actual sportscards from all the major sports. You should take note of how differently the card companies present the information on each player. Try players from the different sports and learn what the abbreviations stand for on each card.

Cartoons/Storyboarding

A story has its life in the imagination. It calls up pictures in the mind, images of action and emotion.

This activity is designed to encourage students to create a storyboard following the action of a favorite story that they have read in class, or to draw a storyboard for a story that they have written themselves.

This activity is related to a comic strip in that only key elements of the plot are shown by the illustrator. However, the story here need not be funny. The students also need to do enough storyboard panels to maintain the sense and integrity of the story.

If some students do not draw well, they can be teamed with students who do. Then the job can be divided into an illustrator and caption writer. At any rate, high quality art work is not the object of these activities. Imagination and creativity should not be sacrificed to any desire to produce better drawings, as long as the students make an honest effort to draw their best and apply their writing skills to create a logical plot and storyboard sequence.

Name _____

Cartoons/Storyboarding

Do you enjoy cartoons and comic strips? Have you ever wondered how they are created? Here is a chance to do one.

Not all comic strips are funny. Many tell a story by breaking the story down into key scenes. These scenes then become individual panels in a storyboard that tells the story.

To do this comic strip:

-1) Pick a favorite story— either one that you have read in class or one you have written yourself.

-2) In correct order, make a list of the key scenes in the story below. Include a description of the scenes and/or any dialogue (spoken words) in the scenes.

Key Scenes in Order

-1)

-2)

-3)

-4)

-5)

-6)

-7)

-8)

-9)

-10)

Name _____

Storyboard Drawing Sheet

Draw your scenes below and put a short description of each on the line below the box. Include any dialogue spoken by the characters.

_____   _____

_____   _____

Name _____

Storyboard Drawing Sheet

Draw your scenes below and put a short description of each on the line below the box. Include any dialogue spoken by the characters.

Name _____

Storyboard Drawing Sheet

Draw your scenes below and put a short description of each on the line below the box. Include any dialogue spoken by the characters.

_____ _____

_____ _____

Name _____

Storyboard Drawing Sheet

Draw your scenes below and put a short description of each on the line below the box. Include any dialogue spoken by the characters.

135

Street Corners

A word to teachers about this project. This is a project that is intended to stimulate students' writing, organization, research, and decision-making skills. However, you can approach it as a project or as a group of activities. Depending on your approach, there is a significant difference in how the work is done and in how much work is done by students.

If the parts of the project are broken down into discrete activities, they can stand alone and function well. If done as a whole, the project offers chances for small group or cooperative learning and for higher level thinking skills.

While there is an implied order to the activities that make up this project, do not feel constrained by this. The main idea is to encourage students to have fun and find out about their local community.

The project's activities are designed to be done as follows:

1) Picture taking or drawing of street corners in the community. (You may want to supply your students with large sheets of paper for this activity.)

2) Give written directions to someone who wishes to travel from one side of your community to the other.

3) Describe a group of "mystery street corners" by writing three clues about each one.

4) Write about a trip around town, describing the sights you see as you go.

Street Corners

Picturing your street corners

For this assignment, you must put together a group of pictures of street corners in our community. You can choose any group of ten street corners that you want to. After you have decided which ten you want to picture, either take a camera and take pictures of them or take a pad of paper and draw what the ten street corners look like. Remember, in creating your pictures include clues to the street names, but do not put street signs in your pictures! Rubber cement or glue your gallery of pictures of street corners to a large sheet of paper.

Name _____

Street Corners

Taking a Trip around Town

Suppose someone wants to take a trip around our town/city. He would need directions on how to get from place to place. Describing the landmarks might help. (For example, "On your right, you will see a big green building.") But, describing the street corners that that person will pass by or through might be even better. Below, give someone directions for a trip from one side of town to another, or a trip of about twelve city blocks, by giving the person a description of the street corners that he will pass through and the names of the streets he will go on. Don't forget to include directions on where to turn and in what direction!

-First pair of street corners/directions

-Second pair of street corners/directions

-Third pair of street corners/directions

-Fourth pair of street corners/directions

-Fifth pair of street corners/directions

Name _____

Street Corners

Mystery Street Corners

Think about ten street corners that you are familiar with. Come up with three "clues" that would identify each one to some one who knows your town, city, or neighborhood. List the ten sets of three clues below. Then exchange them with another group in class. The group with the most solved correctly first and fastest wins! *Your teacher may rule that some clues are not very good ! ! ! Ask her or him if you have any doubts ! !*

-1st set of clues	-2nd set of clues
-3rd set of clues	-4th set of clues
-5th set of clues	-6th set of clues
-7th set of clues	-8th set of clues
-9th set of clues	-10th set of clues

Name _____

Street Corners

Describing a trip around town

Suppose that you wanted to write to a good friend in another town. You wanted to tell that person about your town and the things about it that you see often. You might describe a trip around town in your letter to that friend by naming important landmarks, street corners, or places that you like. Sound like fun? Well that is exactly what you should do below. Remember to put in as many details (landmarks, street corners, places you like) as possible, and describe these things as fully as you can!

140